D1406870

Reading in the Content Areas

Guided Comprehension Practice

Teacher Created Materials
PUBLISHING

Exploring Nonfiction Credits

Published by:
Teacher Created Materials

Publishers:
Rachelle Cracchiolo, M.S. Ed.

Curriculum Product Manager:
Lori Kamola, M.S. Ed.

Editor-in-Chief:
Sharon Coan, M.S. Ed.

Designer:
Lee Aucoin
Phil Garcia

Authors:
Sarah Kartchner Clark, M.A.
Traci Clausen
Debra J. Housel, M.S. Ed.
Kathleen Kehl Lewis, M.A. Ed.
Jennifer Overend Prior, M. Ed.
Jan Ray, Ed. D.
Andrea Trischitta, M.A./M.A.T.

Editorial Staff:
Carol Bloch, M.A. Ed.
Sharon Coan, M.S. Ed.
Marshall Grodin, M.J.
Lori Kamola, M.S. Ed.

Production:
Phil Garcia
Alfred Lau

TIME For Kids® Credits

Publisher:
Keith Garton

Executive Editor:
Jonathan Rosenbloom

Writer:
Curtis Slepian

Photo Editor:
Bettina Stammen

Table of Contents

THE CITY NEWS

MAIL PAGE

We welcome mail from readers. These two letters are about our article: "Violence in the Media: Too Much?"

Dear City News,

I totally agree with your article about violence. I think there is too much violence on TV and in the movies. People are always fighting and shooting on police and detective shows. The TV news shows too many violent stories.

Cartoon shows are just as bad. They have a lot of violence. Even the animals fight. The problem is lots of kids watch cartoons. It teaches them bad lessons.

Movies are even worse. First of all, they are more real looking and more violent than TV. Second, the movie rating system doesn't keep little kids out of movies with "ordinary" violence.

Video games are also far too violent. Like movies, video games are rated for age level. But if a teenager buys a game for his age level, a young child can easily get to play it.

People tend to copy what they see. If they see violent things, they will become violent. We are surrounded with these violent pictures. After a while, we get used to it.

We need to do more than just give ratings to TV, movies, and video games. There should be laws to prevent them from being released.

James Wilton
Cranston, NJ

Dear City News,

Your story on violence was totally wrong. Here's why. No one has proven that violent pictures make people act violently. Many studies say it just isn't true. If you read history, you'll see that people have always acted violently. Violence will exist even if no one sees a movie or TV show.

I disagree with the article on another point. The writer says the government should outlaw violence on TV and in the movies. I say the Constitution gives us freedom of speech. You can't forbid things just because you're against them. Pretty soon, people will ban things that you are for.

If you don't like violent things, don't watch them. But don't stop other people from making their own free choices.

Alice Reynolds
Little Falls, NJ

Notes

A Sweet Science

Donna Zeller Gets Paid To Have Good Taste

By Angelique Siniawski

Too sour? Too sweet? Just right? Zeller and her team sample foods at a tasting meeting.

Chocolate candy bars, fresh peanuts and almonds, cocoa beans, watermelon-flavored candy. Sound tasty? Donna Zeller gets paid to taste treats like these every day. You see, Zeller is a sensory scientist for Hershey Foods. Her job is to taste chocolate and study test results. "Chocolate is a complex flavor," says Zeller.

Zeller has worked at Hershey for 13 years. "We make sure that our candy bars remain the same over time," she says. When someone bites into a candy bar, that person expect a certain taste. Making chocolate bars taste exactly the same every time isn't easy. That's because some ingredients can have a different taste from season to season. This is true of peanuts and cocoa beans.

What Is Chocolate?

Chocolate is made from cocoa beans. There are many different types of cocoa beans. They are grown in many different countries. Chocolate makers must blend different beans together. They do it to give their chocolate the same taste bar after bar. Then it's up to tasters like Zeller to decide if their bars taste just right.

The Taste Test

To pick the perfect ingredients, the tasters need a good sense of smell and taste. Special taste cells on the tongue give us four basic tastes: sweet, salty, bitter, and sour. "Everything else is a combination of smelling and tasting," explains Zeller. Want proof? Mix some sugar and cinnamon. Hold your nose and taste the mixture. You taste the sweet sugar. Now let go of your nostrils. Your sense of smell helps you taste the cinnamon. "Tasting is a science," says Zeller. She should know—she studied biology in college.

Believe it or not, tasters never get too full. The key to tasting is spitting out. "If you swallowed everything, you'd be sick" says Zeller. "We carry spit cups with us."

Chocolate Troubles

You may have noticed that the price of chocolate is going up. One reason is that there is less chocolate coming from Brazil. That's because Brazil's cacao trees are sick. The trees grow the beans from which chocolate is made. In 2000, the bean harvest was the smallest in 30 years.

Brazil's farmers are trying to save the trees by spraying chemicals on them. Early results say the treatments are working.

What does this mean for chocolate lovers? As the supply of chocolate goes down, the price goes up. So keep your fingers crossed that the problem will be solved soon.

A healthy cocoa bean (left) and a sick one (above).

ALVARO DE LEIVA/LIAISON

Notes

7

Seuss on the Loose

Over here, over there, suddenly Seuss is everywhere!

By Rita Upadhyay

Jim Carrey as the Grinch. Next to him is Taylor Momnsen, who plays Cindy-Lou Who.

Oh, the places we'll all go! Audiences have packed theaters to see the movie version of *How the Grinch Stole Christmas*. That classic tale was written by Dr. Seuss. The movie's sky-high ticket sales prove that the doctor is still in—and not just for movie lovers. Seuss-mania is sweeping the country.

Another Seuss-y place to visit is Seuss Landing at Universal Island of Adventure in Orlando, Florida. There, you can ride around with the Cat in the Hat. A full cast of Seuss characters marched onstage when *Seussical the Musical* opened on Broadway. Seuss's favorite cat is also set to star in his own movie.

What's behind this big Seuss comeback? It may be his wife, Audrey Geisel. She spent her life taking care of the beloved author. Dr. Seuss, whose real name was Theodor Seuss Geisel, died in 1991. Since then, Audrey Geisel must approve anything made from his stories. Nothing goes to screen, stage, or stores without her OK. She even met with actor Jim Carrey before *How the Grinch Stole Christmas* started filming. When they met, Carrey, who plays the Grinch, didn't shake her hand. Instead, he spun her around, held her close, and made a Grinch face. Geisel was sold.

Carrey grew up loving Seuss's holiday fable. "In a very simple tale, Seuss tells you a lot about the way humans behave," he says.

How would the good doctor have handled today's Seuss-popularity? "If Ted were here," Audrey Geisel told the Seussical cast, "his heart would have grown three sizes."

TOP SIX

Here is a list of six popular Dr. Suess books. How many have you read?

The Cat in the Hat

One Fish Two Fish Red Fish Blue Fish

Green Eggs and Ham

How the Grinch Stole Christmas

Oh, The Places You'll Go

The Foot Book

Theodor Seuss Geisel sits with his wife, Audrey.

Notes

MIA HAMM

ERIK PEREL/ALLSPORT

Mia Hamm is one of the greatest soccer players ever. Her drive to be the best started when she was young.

Hamm was born in Selma, Alabama, in 1972. She is shy, but not when she plays games. Even as a child, Hamm always wanted to win. She has said, "I quit a lot of games because I hated losing so much." Eventually, her four brothers and sisters wouldn't let her play unless she stayed to the end. Hamm started playing soccer at age seven. After that, she never again quit during a game.

A Gift for Soccer

Hamm quickly became very good at soccer. When she was 14, the coach of women's soccer at the University of North Carolina talked her into coming to his school. Hamm's college team won four straight NCAA soccer championships. By the time she graduated, she had set many records, including most points, most goals, and most assists in women's college soccer history.

Since graduating, Hamm has been a star player for the U.S. National Team. In 1991, the team won the first women's World Championship in China. Hamm, at age 19, was the youngest player on the team. She has been recognized as the greatest woman soccer player in the world. She is fast and aggressive and scores many goals. Hamm was the MVP in the women's World Cup in 1995 and 1997. She played in two Olympics, winning gold and silver medals. Currently, she plays in the first women's pro soccer league, the WUSA. Hamm stars at forward for the Washington Freedom.

Another Goal

But Hamm's life isn't just about sports. Her adopted brother died of a blood disease. So she sponsored soccer all-star games to raise money to fight bone-marrow disease. At one game, she brought together the people who had received bone marrow and people who donated theirs to them. Hamm said, "This was my most satisfying moment away from the field."

KEY DATES:

- **March 17, 1972** born in Selma, Alabama
- **1987** became the youngest player (at age 15) on the U.S. national women's soccer team
- **1994** had her number retired at the University of North Carolina
- **1994–1998** was named U.S. Soccer Federation Female Athlete of the Year for five straight years
- **1996** won an Olympic Gold medal in Atlanta, Georgia
- **1998** was voted ESPY Sportswoman of the Year
- **1999** was the world's leading goal scorer in international competition, male or female

Notes

The City News

Sanitation Department's New Plan Is a Lot of Garbage

DAVID SAILORS/CORBIS STOCK MARKET

Not in Kennedy Elementary's backyard

The Department of Sanitation's site for a new town dump is a big mistake. According to the plan, the landfill will be built about 150 yards from Kennedy Elementary School. It is the largest elementary school in the county. Work on the dump will be finished by the start of the new school year. Commissioner of the Sanitation Department, John Laury, says the dump will be 14,000 square yards. It will be able to hold 48,000 tons of garbage. The old dump outside Colbyville is full.

A Health Hazard

Getting rid of our garbage is a big problem. But we think this dump is the wrong solution. The new dump will be much too close to the school. It is possible that children on the way to and from school might go into the dump and fall in. They might become sick because of the rotting food.

In addition, the smell from the dump will be terrible. The Colbyville dump gives off a nasty odor. Imagine this smell going through the windows of Kennedy Elementary— especially in warm weather. It will be very hard for students to think and study because of that stink.

An Illegal Sale?

Why was this property picked for the dump? Last week an article in this newspaper gave the reason: The city bought the land from the sanitation commissioner's brother, Fred Laury. He made a huge amount of money from that sale. Commissioner John Laury says he didn't realize that land was owned by his brother. His explanation stinks! We don't believe him. We don't think the voters will believe him when the next election comes up. We call for a full investigation of this trashy situation.

Dump the Garbage Plan

We ask the mayor to step in. He must use his power to change the location of the dump. Move it to Shelbyville. Or to Bay Ridge. Just don't move it near Kennedy Elementary School.

Notes

13

The Dreams of Rats

New Research May Unlock Clues to Human Dreams

By Eric Rudolph

(Boston, Massachusetts, February 2) A new study says that rats have dreams about their everyday lives. The study also said rats remember more than anyone thought.

JEFFMOORES

Scientists say that dreams may help rats do better during waking hours.

Dreaming of Mazes

Scientists found that sleeping rats dream about the mazes they've run through when they're awake. How did scientists figure this out? They attached special instruments to the rats. (These do not hurt the rats.) The instruments measured brain waves while the rats were asleep. Then researchers measured the brain waves when the rats were awake and running through the maze.

Then scientists compared both brain-wave patterns. They discovered that the patterns matched. They were so similar that researchers believed the rats were dreaming of the maze. In fact, the researchers say they can tell exactly what part of a maze the rat is dreaming of.

Figuring It Out

These brain waves come from a certain part of the brain. This area handles memory. Dreaming may help the rats memorize the complicated paths.

Rats' brains are like human brains. That's why scientists say this study could help us learn more about the human mind. "It's really opening a new door into the study of dreams," said Professor Matt Wilson. He worked on the project at the University of Massachusetts. Scientists say humans solve problems in

dreams. They also say that dreams help us hold onto memories longer.

Further Proof

This research supports what other tests have shown. Scientists at the University of Chicago did a similar experiment. They tested songbirds the same way rats were tested. Researchers attached electrodes to the birds and checked their brain patterns while singing and while sleeping. They found that song birds dream about their singing.

Notes

POOL SAFETY

Swimming pools are fun places. But they can also be dangerous. Many accidents happen in and around pools. So learn these few, important safety tips. Then pass them along to your family—you'll make a big splash.

1. Learn to swim. It will make being around water much safer—and more enjoyable. To learn how to swim, enroll at your local YMCA or community pool.

2. Never swim anywhere without an adult watching you. If there's trouble in the water, you will need an adult to help you. It is also a good idea to have a swimming buddy with you in the water, too.

3. Some pools have covers over them. They keep out leaves and dirt, as well as small kids. Never swim if the cover is partly on. You could get trapped underneath it.

4. There should always be a phone at or very near poolside. Or adults should be carrying cell phones. Emergency numbers must be posted right by the phone so that help can be called right away.

5. Diving can be very dangerous. Never dive into a pool that's less than nine feet deep. Also, don't dive into a pool built above ground. They are too shallow. If a pool is built below ground, don't dive from the side. Instead, enter the water feet first. If you know how to dive, do it only from the deep end of the pool—the side with a diving board. If you know how to dive, be sure your hands are in front of you. Always steer up as you enter the water, so you don't hit the bottom. If you use a pool slide, never slide head first. Always go feet first.

6. When you're in the water, don't push or dunk swimmers.

7. Be sure lifesaving equipment is near poolside. There should be a pole, life preservers, and rope. Hang them on a fence so people won't trip on them.

8. Don't fool around and scream for help if you don't really need it. A false alarm may make people ignore a real emergency.

9. Don't swim during thunderstorms. There's always a chance you could get struck by lightning.

10. Don't bring glass poolside. If it breaks, people with bare feet might get badly cut.

Notes

Fresh Start in Africa

A Special Boarding School in
Kenya Gives Troubled Boys
Another Chance
By Andrew Goldstein

Brandon Harlee left behind this rough neighborhood in Baltimore, Maryland.

Brandon Harlee grew up in a tough neighborhood in Baltimore, Maryland. It was filled with drugs and gangs. Even little kids learned to act tough there. By sixth grade, Brandon had become too much for his mom and his school to handle. He earned bad grades and was always fighting.

Then Brandon got an amazing chance to change his life. Thanks to an unusual program, he was sent to a school in Africa. For Brandon, things didn't start well in Africa. But soon he began to climb trees, collect bugs, do homework, read—and learn.

A New Beginning

Robert Embry got the idea for the school in Africa. He works for a group that tries to help Baltimore schools. He asked school principals what they needed most. They said some students made it tough for the others to learn. The principals wanted to get help for those troublemakers.

So Embry's group set up a new school in the African nation of Kenya. The school was named Baraka. This word means "blessing" in Swahili, an African language. Half of Baraka's teachers are Kenyan. The other half are American. The boys are chosen because they have problems in school but show some promise. Brandon had never brought a single book home from school. At Baraka, he had to take hard classes to catch up.

A Tough Start

Brandon started out talking back to his teachers. His punishment was having to live outside in a tent. Brandon soon learned that staying out of trouble would earn him neat stuff—safaris (trips to see animals in the wild), video nights, and visits to Kenya's capital, Nairobi.

When the boys return to the U.S., they are placed in a good public school or Embry's group pays for a private school.

Brandon thinks what he learned at Baraka was important. "I learned not to be a ringleader or a crowd follower," he says. He finished seventh and eight grades in Kenya and was named Most Improved Student. Now Brandon is in high school in Baltimore. He got an A+ on his first Latin test!

Brandon and a Baraka classmate get a lesson from a member of a local tribe.

Notes

A Woman Up a Tree

Redwood Seriously Damaged After Attempts to Save It

By Iris Rose

(Stafford, California, December 8) Julia Hill's nickname is Butterfly. Like real butterflies, Hill has spent a lot of time up in the air. For two years, she lived in the branches of a 200-foot-tall redwood tree. Hill climbed the tree as a protest. She was against loggers cutting down redwood trees in Northern California. She said, "Here I can be the voice and face of this tree."

It was a tough two years for Hill, but her sacrifice paid off. She came down after a lumber company said it wouldn't touch the 1,000-year-old giant tree.

New Danger

But now the tree is in even bigger danger. Someone—no one knows who—has cut deep into the tree's trunk with a chain saw. This cut has made the tree weak and unstable.

Experts say it could be blown over by strong winter storms. Recently, Hill visited the tree, which she named Luna. She touched the 32-inch gash and said, "I feel this vicious attack on Luna as if

SHAUN WALKER/EUREKA TIMES-STANDARD/AP

Experts reach around the giant tree to measure the damage.

the chain saw was going through me."

Life in a Tree

Hill feels strongly about the tree. When she came down from it after two years, she was sad: "I just felt like my heart was being ripped out." The tree, she said, "was the best friend I've ever had." While on Luna, Hill lived in a 6-foot by 8-foot treehouse. She had no shower. Friends sent up food in buckets. She had to cook the food on a small gas-burning stove. She kept in shape by climbing the branches of the 18-story-high tree.

Hill spent most of her time in the tree talking on a cell phone. For six to eight hours a day, she gave interviews and explained what she was doing to school students. She got 300 letters every week from people all over the world. Most mentioned how much Hill inspired them by helping Luna.

Hope for Luna

Now, Hill must go to Luna's aid again. The redwood isn't dead, but it needs help to survive. An emergency team has put steel braces over the cut. These will support the tree. Hill belongs to an environmental group called Circle of Life Foundation. It is working with experts to figure out how to save the tree permanently.

Hill is not giving up. "I am as committed as ever to protect Luna and the remaining ancient forests."

Julia ("Butterfly") Hill checks the braces holding up the tree.

Notes

Editorial Page

The City News

Our Future Is in the Stars

Thirty years ago there was great interest in exploring our solar system. In those days we were excited to send men to the moon. But today our government seems to think exploring—and colonizing—other worlds is not important.

We disagree. We think the time has come to boost our space program. The International Space Station and space shuttle are fine. But they don't go far enough. We believe that astronauts must be sent back to the moon and then to Mars. We must build colonies on those worlds and on the moons of Jupiter and Saturn.

HULTON ARCHIVE

Exploring Is in Our Blood

Humans are explorers. It is in our blood. Explorers took chances to reach the New World. They took chances hiking across the North and South poles for the first time.

People don't explore just for material rewards. Humans explore to get new information about the world. Right now we need new information about the planets and moons of our solar system. This information will help explain the universe and our place in it. But exploring isn't enough. We should also build colonies on these worlds. Earth's resources are dwindling. New worlds will provide us with new resources.

Bringing Nations Together

There is another good thing about these projects. Many countries will have to work together to explore and settle the solar system. This cooperation will, no doubt, create a more peaceful planet Earth.

Our new age of exploration should begin with the moon. NASA and the space agencies of other nations must send humans there. Then we should build a permanent colony.

The next target will be Mars. Some scientists say there may be water on Mars—below its surface. This water would be the key to making Mars liveable for humans. It would take a long time before humans can settle on Mars. But we should try to make it so. We believe Congress must give NASA more money. After all, our future is in the stars.

Notes

SOLVING PROBLEMS

Making Decisions

"Cool!" said Jamal. He was walking into the Trading Card Show. "I've got $20 to buy cards. What will I spend it on?"

Choice #1
All-Star Baseball Cards
$2.50 for 1 pack
3 packs for $7.00

Choice #2
Goofy Joke Cards
25 cards in a big bag
3 bags in a package
$10.25 for a package

Choice #3
Sci-Fi Cards
$1.75 a pack
6 packs for the price of 5
8 packs for the price of 7

Your Turn

1. How many cards do you get in a big bag of Goofy Joke cards?

2. How many cards do you get in a package of Goofy Joke cards?

3. How much do 6 packs of Sci-Fi cards cost?

4. Which costs more: one pack of Baseball cards or one pack of Sci-Fi cards? How much more?

Making Choices

5. How much would Jamal pay for 8 packs of Sci-Fi cards?

6. Jamal buys a package of Goofy Joke cards. He pays with his $20 bill. How much change does he get back?

7. Jamal chooses to buy 6 packs of All-Star Baseball cards. How much will it cost Jamal? How much does he save if he buys them in packs?

8. If Jamal wants to buy 8 packs of Sci-Fi cards and a package of Goofy Joke cards, will he be able to? Why or why not?

Notes

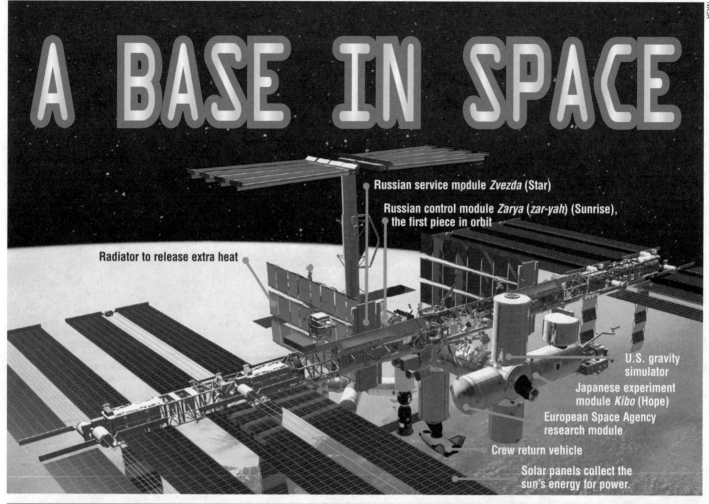

A BASE IN SPACE

Russian service module *Zvezda* (Star)

Russian control module *Zarya* (*zar-yah*) (Sunrise), the first piece in orbit

Radiator to release extra heat

U.S. gravity simulator

Japanese experiment module *Kibo* (Hope)

European Space Agency research module

Crew return vehicle

Solar panels collect the sun's energy for power.

How the Completed Station Will Look

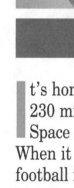

Science

It's home sweet home. Except this home is 230 miles above Earth! The International Space Station won't be finished until 2006. When it is completed, it will be as long as two football fields. That will make the station the biggest human-made object ever to float in space.

Sixteen nations, including the U.S. and Russia, have worked together to build the lab. Right now, a team of astronauts is busy building the station. While they work, they're staying in a small living section called *Zvezda* (*zvez-dah*). (That's the Russian word for "star.") Their little home has food, water, a machine to make oxygen so they can breathe easily, laptop computers, exercise machines— even a high-tech toilet!

The pieces of the space station are being sent from Earth. It will take more than 40 trips to get all the stuff up in space. Once the pieces are up there, it's pretty easy to put them together. That's because the gravity in space is very low. Materials that weigh tons on Earth are light as a feather in orbit.

When the International Space Station is complete, astronauts on board will do experiments. They will see if being weightless for a long time affects their health. They hope to invent things that work better in low gravity. One day, the space station may be a launching pad for a mission to Mars and other planets. No wonder astronauts are sky high about the future of the International Space Station!

Notes

Arctic Wildlife

A fight is taking place in Alaska over the Arctic National Wildlife Refuge. Many people want to drill for oil there. Others fear that the drilling will disturb the animals that live in this beautiful wilderness area. The Arctic National Wildlife Refuge is home to many different animals. Some live in the Arctic Ocean. Many others live in the Arctic tundra, a treeless area of land. The chart below describes some of these cold-weather animals.

Animal	Features	Average Male Weight	Food	Where They Live
 Polar Bear	thick fur; webbed feet; sharp claws	1,000 pounds	seals	Arctic ice; coastlines
 Caribou	thick fur; sharp hooves; short body	550 pounds	moss; leaves; twigs	tundra
 Musk Ox	long, brown fur; large, wide hooves; short body	600 pounds	tree branches; bushes; grass	tundra
 Arctic Seal	gray fur; blubber; flippers	175 pounds	plankton (small ocean life)	Arctic Ocean

JOANNA MCCARTHY/IMAGE BANK

FLIP CHALFANT/IMAGE BANK

TERJE RAKKE/ IMAGE BANK

EASTCOTT/MOMATIUK/STONE

Science

Notes

FORCES OF THE EARTH:
Undersea Volcanoes

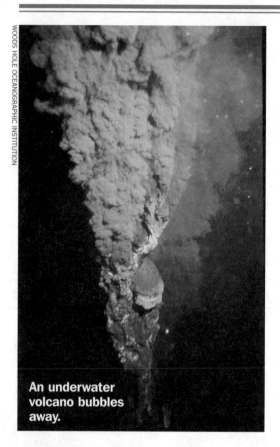

An underwater volcano bubbles away.

Some of the biggest volcanoes on Earth have never been seen by humans. That's because they're very deep underwater. You'd have to dive down a mile and a half just to reach the tops of these volcanoes. This string of underwater volcanoes is called the Mid-Ocean Ridge.

The Mid-Ocean Ridge is the biggest mountain range on our planet. It's more than 30,000 miles long and almost 500 miles wide. Its hundreds of mountains and volcanoes zigzag under the ocean between the continents. They wind their way around the globe like the seam on a baseball. That means there are underwater mountains and volcanoes all around the world. Nearly every day, at least one underwater volcano erupts. Super-hot lava pours out of the volcano and onto the ocean floor.

The bottom of the sea is always changing. Super-hot lava erupts from deep inside the Earth. Then the lava cools, forming rocks. Layers of rocky lava pile up. Over millions of years, all that lava makes the sea floor expand. As the sea floor expands, it pushes the continents around. A million years ago, the Earth looked very different than it does today. A million years from now, it will have changed even more.

The Mid-Ocean Ridge (shown in red) winds its way between the continents like the seam on a baseball. Do you live near the Mid-Ocean Ridge?

ISLAND POPPING

When volcanoes erupt underwater, they can form a mountain of lava. If the mountain reaches the surface of the sea, it often forms a volcanic island. That's how Surtsey, the world's newest land mass, was created. Surtsey first appeared in 1963 off the coast of Iceland (an island nation in the Atlantic Ocean). The erupting volcano had risen 300 feet from the bottom of the ocean. Icelanders named the volcanic island Surtsey. That's the name of the god of fire in their mythology. For three and a half years, lava kept flowing from Surtsey. By the time the volcano stopped erupting in 1967, the island was a mile wide and 560 feet high.

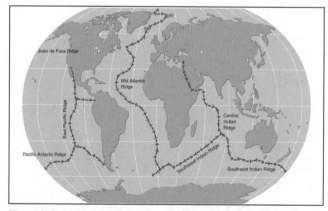

Notes

31

DAVID YOUNG WOLFF/STONE

Recycling Is Right!

If you think recycling is a lot of garbage, you're right. Recycling allows us to change tons of garbage back into new metal, plastic, glass, and paper products. You and your family can help the environment by recycling. Just follow these recycling rules.

Recycling Rules

● **Four kinds of materials can be recycled: paper, metal, plastic, and glass products. But you can't recycle just anything. Here is a list of some things that can and can't be recycled:**

YES! Recycle these paper materials: cardboard, magazines, catalogs, newspapers, writing paper, envelopes, paper bags, computer paper, and clean pizza boxes.

NO! Don't recycle: shiny candy wrappers, paper towels, and napkins.

YES! Recycle these metal, plastic, and glass products: milk and juice cartons, metal cans, plastic and glass bottles, and milk jugs.

NO! Don't recycle: plastic straws, toys, craft projects, deli containers, plastic utensils, and Styrofoam®.

● **Before you recycle, rinse bottles, jugs, and cans. Aluminum foil used for cooking should also be washed.**

● **Place paper products in a bag or can labeled for holding this type of material.**

● **Place glass, plastic, and metal items in another container labeled for holding these materials.**

● **Don't place so much in one can that it overflows. Don't overfill bags—they may break and create litter.**

● **Bundle up and tie cardboard separately.**

● **Find out when the recycling collector comes to your house. Before the collector arrives, place the bags, cans, and cardboard on the curb for pick up.**

Notes

SHIPWRECK: The tanker *Jessica* ran aground, spilling oil.

The Galapagos Islands Face a Sticky Situation

By Andrea Dorfman

GALAPAGOS ISLANDS, February 2—A ship carrying 240,000 gallons of oil struck an underwater object off an island in the Galapagos chain. The ship, Jessica, tipped over and began leaking oil. The fuel has spread over an area larger than the city of Los Angeles.

The animals who live in this group of islands, located about 600 miles off the coast of Ecuador, are in serious danger from the spill. Penguins, sea lions, giant tortoises, and lizards that call the islands home may suffer from the spill. Scientists say the islands' animals could get coated with oil or poisoned by eating it. Hundreds of volunteers are helping clean up the gooey black mess. It could take at least two years to complete the job.

Rescue workers treat the oily animals like babies, using gentle soap to wash fur and feathers. They use milk, which doesn't sting the animals' eyes, to clean their heads.

The weather has helped out, too. "We have had luck because the sea currents, the winds and the sun have kept the spill from causing major damage," said Fernando Espinoza. He's the director of a Galapagos conservation group.

The Human Threat

Oil spills are not the only danger to the Galapagos. People are a danger, too. More and more tourists visit the Galapagos every year. The islands have been protected as a national park since 1959. But that may not be enough. Unless more is done to protect the islands from people and from shipping accidents, it may be too late to save this one-of-a-kind habitat.

ECUADOR   *Equator*

GALAPAGOS ISLANDS   Fuel Tanker Spill

Equator

SOUTH AMERICA

PACIFIC OCEAN

ATLANTIC OCEAN

0 MILES 50   SAN CRISTOBAL ISLAND

PACIFIC OCEAN

Rescue workers gently try to wash oil from a pelican.

Notes

THE CORAL REEF CRISIS

People, pollution, and warming waters are a danger to underwater reefs around the world.

By Ritu Upadhyay

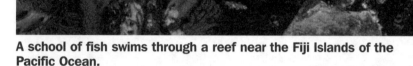

A school of fish swims through a reef near the Fiji Islands of the Pacific Ocean.

Pollution has caused sea plants to strangle the reef above. Warm water has bleached the reef at left.

NORBERT WU

Under the clear blue sea, busy groups of ocean creatures live together in brightly colored structures. These beautiful underwater cities are called coral reefs, and they have been around for millions of years.

But danger looms. Last month, scientists gave a strong warning. Pollution and careless humans have destroyed more than a quarter of the world's reefs. If things don't improve quickly, all the reefs may die in the next 20 years. That would put thousands of sea creatures at risk of dying out.

Precious Habitats

Coral seems like rock because of its stone-like surface. But it is actually made up of tiny clear animals called **coral polyps** (*poll-ups*). Many are less than one inch wide. Millions of coral polyps stick together in colonies and form a hard shell. As colonies grow together, they make big reefs. The bright color of coral comes from tiny sea plants called **algae** (*al-gee*). Coral and algae depend on each other to live. This is called **symbiosis** (sim-bee-oh-sis).

Coral may feel tough, but it's very sensitive. Pollution has hurt many reefs. Bad fishing methods, including the use of dynamite to shock fish, have also caused terrible harm.

Warming Waters

But the biggest threat is that oceans are getting warmer. Warm water causes coral to lose the algae that provide its food and color. This deadly process is called **coral bleaching**.

It's Time to Help

Scientists believe that the reefs can still be saved if governments outlaw bad practices and control pollution. "The world's attitude must change," says scientist Clive Wilkinson. Maybe it already has. Recently, a group called the United Nations Foundation said it would give 10 million dollars to help save the reefs. The money will be used to study reefs and teach people how to help.

WORD WATCH

Algae—sea plants that give food and color to coral

Coral bleaching—harmful process caused by warm water; it destroys reefs by making them lose their color and food supply

Coral polyps—tiny animals that join together to form coral reefs

Symbiosis—when two plants and/or animals live together and depend on each other for survival

Notes

Fire Safety: A Hot Idea

ROBERT LANDEAU/CORBIS

Every year, thousands of Americans die in fires that take place in their homes. Do you know what you would do in a fire? Share these fire safety tips with your parents. One day, the tips may save your lives.

1. Be sure your house has a smoke alarm. This will give you an early warning about fires. Alarms should be near all the bedrooms. Test them once a month to be sure the batteries work. Replace the batteries every six months.

2. Plan an escape route for the whole family—before the fire strikes. Fires can make you too confused and panicky to think straight. A plan will help you get out fast. You should have two ways to get out of every room. If a fire blocks one path, you can escape by another path.

3. Practice your escape route once a month. A smoky fire can make it hard to see. So when you practice, turn the lights off in your house or walk with your eyes closed.

4. If a fire does strike, leave the house right away. Don't grab any objects, no matter how important they are to you.

5. Smoke and flames rise. It will be easier to breathe low to the ground. So stay down.

6. Before you open a door, touch the door or doorknob with your hand. If it's hot, it means the fire is on the other side. Take a different escape path.

7. Once you're out of the house, meet your family at a safe spot chosen beforehand. It should be fairly close to the house. This way, you'll know who has escaped and who hasn't.

8. Call 911 or the fire department immediately. It is best to call from a neighbor's house.

9. Never go back into a burning building. Tell the firefighters if a person or pet is missing.

Notes

MAMMALS
The World of Primates: Apes and Monkeys

On the surface, apes, monkeys, and humans aren't much alike. There are 14 kinds of apes and 158 kinds of monkeys. Some weigh more than 600 pounds, and some are as small as a mouse. Then there are humans—animals that walk upright and talk. We're very different from one another. But we have one thing in common: We're all primates!

What Makes a Primate?

First of all, primates are mammals. They have warm blood and fur. Primates are also social animals. They enjoy time with friends and family. Instead of paws, primates have hands. Many even have thumbs and fingernails. Most primates are good climbers. They grab and swing using their hands and feet. A few use long tails to help them climb.

Where Primates Hang Out

Most primates come from warm places in Africa, South America, and Asia. Many live in jungles and rain forests. There they play together, swing and run through trees, search for food, and look out for dangerous animals like snakes, eagles, and tigers.

Sometimes, though, primates live in zoos. Away from their home, they could get bored and upset. Zoo keepers build special climbing walls, add new toys and games, and bring surprises to keep the primates happy and interested.

GORILLA

GIBBON

CHIMPANZEE

ORANGUTAN

ART WOLFE/STONE
ART WOLFE/STONE
MANOJ SHAH/STONE
MANOJ SHAH/STONE

Some Great Apes

As primates, monkeys and apes have a lot in common. But they also have a few differences. Unlike monkeys, apes have no tail and can walk upright for a short time. Apes are generally smarter than monkeys. Here are the four main types of apes:

GORILLAS: The biggest primates in the world, they weigh up to 650 pounds. These gentle giants live in West Africa, where they eat nuts and leaves.

GIBBONS: They live in the treetops of the Far East and Southeast Asia. Their long arms let them swing amazingly fast from branch to branch. One type of gibbon yells so loudly, it can be heard a mile away.

CHIMPANZEES: Chimpanzees travel in groups throughout the forests and grasslands of Africa. Chimpanzees are so smart, they have a language. Instead of words, they use sounds and facial expressions.

ORANGUTAN: The second-biggest ape, it can weigh up to 200 pounds. These intelligent, red-furred apes live in the rain forests of Borneo and Sumatra. In fact, they almost never come down from their branches.

Notes

The West Is Burning

Firefighters battle to put out flames.

By Ritu Upadhyay

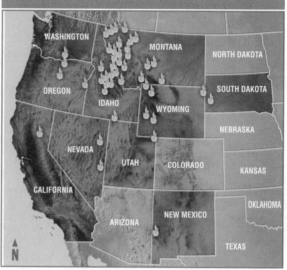

HOT SPOTS

Red-hot flames crept closer and closer to Christopher Atherly's home. Firefighters told him and his family to leave their house in Red Lodge, Montana. Christopher, who is 8, packed up his toys. "I was really scared," he says. "I was thinking about how fast the fire was moving and what it would be like if our house burned down."

A Terrible Fire

Hundreds of families across the West are running away from the worst forest fires in 50 years. Right now, huge fires are burning in 10 states (*see map*). This year, fires have destroyed 6.3 million acres. That's an area as big as Vermont! Last week rain slowed down some of the fires, but it didn't put them out. Experts believe the fires will burn until October, when heavier rain and snowfall set in.

Wildfires are a natural part of the life cycle of forests. They help clear dead trees and make way for new growth. But very dry weather and lightning storms have caused the fires to spread out of control.

The Brave Battle

More than 26,000 firefighters, 1,200 fire engines and 240 helicopters are on the job. The cost of fighting the fires is expected to be more than $1 billion. "Everybody is exhausted," says firefighter Murray Taylor.

Fires are always a threat to people who live near forests in the western U.S. Still, many families love living there. "We've decided that if we lose our place, we're going to rebuild it," says Bob Fritzel of Black Hills, South Dakota.

Dry weather has allowed wildfires to spread very quickly. Firefighters can't keep up with them.

DEBRA REID/SPARKS TRIBUNE/CORBIS SYGMA

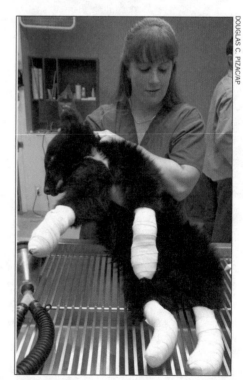

DOUGLAS C. PIZAC/AP

Many animals have been hurt by the flames. This cub's paws were burned.

Notes

Spin Cycle:
How a Hurricane Works

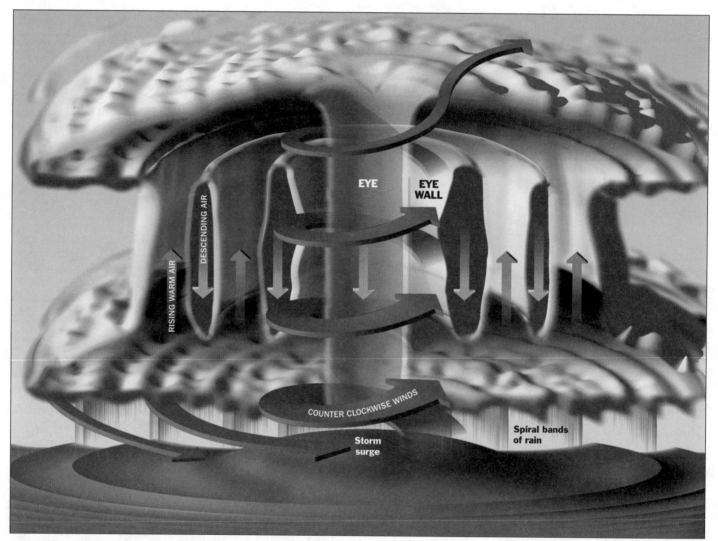

EYE

EYE WALL

DESCENDING AIR

RISING WARM AIR

COUNTER CLOCKWISE WINDS

Storm surge

Spiral bands of rain

The center of the storm is called the eye. This is a column of calm air. Powerful winds are spinning around the eye. The strongest winds form the inner wall of the eye. Giant clouds swirl around the eye. They cause large amounts of rain and lightning.

A hurricane is a big wind machine. How do you build one? Make some thunderstorms and get them to move in a big circle. The best time to make a hurricane is late summer. That's when the ocean water is warmest. The warm air over the ocean rises and creates fierce thunderstorms. Sometimes, many of these storms combine. If the storms begin to spin in the same direction, a hurricane can form.

Super Winds
When the spinning winds reach 74 miles per hour (mph), the storm is called a hurricane. The winds of a hurricane can reach speeds up to 180 mph. When a hurricane hits land, it often causes great destruction. One reason is that a hurricane raises the sea level, flooding the coastline. This can send a 30-foot wall of water inland!

Notes

JOSE LUIS PELAEZ INC./THE STOCK MARKET

I Feel Sooo Sick!

It's time to get out of bed and get ready for school, but you just can't do it. Your skin feels warm to the touch and you feel lightheaded. You ask yourself, "What's making me sick?"

Read the chart for information about common illnesses that can cause you to stay home from school.

Illness	Symptoms	Prevention	Treatment	Did You Know?
Chicken Pox	tiredness; slight fever; no appetite; flat red spots that turn into pimples	Keep away from infected people. Get the chicken-pox vaccine.	A doctor will tell you when to use a non-aspirin fever reducer and how to deal with itching.	It's rare to get chicken pox more than once.
Common Cold	runny nose; congestion; sneezing; sometimes fever; sore throat; tiredness; lack of appetite	Keep away from infected people. Eat a balanced diet. Get plenty of rest. Exercise. Wash your hands often.	There is no known cure for a cold. Get plenty of rest and drink lots of fluids.	Doctors think there are more than 1,500 different kinds of cold viruses or virus combinations.
Flu (Influenza)	sudden fever (sometimes with chills and shaking); aches and tiredness	Keep away from infected people. A flu shot and washing your hands can often help.	Rest, drink fluids, and eat a nutritious diet. An adult may suggest you take a non-aspirin fever reducer.	When you cough or sneeze, a flu virus can travel up to 25 feet away.
Food Poisoning	headaches; chills; upset stomach and weakness	Cook and handle food properly. Choose clean restaurants and markets.	Tell a doctor, especially if symptoms don't go away.	Some scientists think more than 6 million people get sick each year from the food they eat.

Notes

Cities and the Environment

Can Venice Be Saved?

Flooding makes walking in Venice an adventure.

No city on Earth can match beautiful Venice, Italy. Built on 118 islands, it is a place where canals serve as streets and boats serve as taxis. But one of the very things that makes Venice special—its waterways—is harming the city.

Venice is sinking. The city was built on soft, marshy land in a **lagoon**, or shallow body of water.

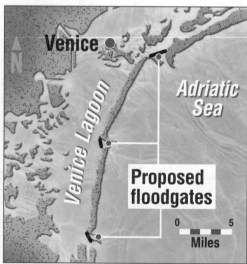

PROJECT MOSES: Huge floodgates would be built at the entrances to the lagoon. The gates would lift up from the ocean floor and block the seawater.

Over the years, the buildings have been sinking. Meanwhile, climate changes have caused the nearby Adriatic Sea to rise. So, seawater often floods the city.

The Problem

Each year, from October to March, strong winds and high tides cause terrible floods. The floods can destroy homes and businesses. The seawater has damaged art treasures and **historic** buildings. Some experts say Venice will sink eight inches in the next 50 years.

A Plan to Save the City

A group wants to save Venice. It has come up with a $2 billion plan to stop the flooding. The plan is called Project Moses. Huge underwater gates would be placed at the three entrances to the Venice lagoon (see map). The gates would act as dams and hold back the seawater.

Some people believe that the gates would be harmful. They say that shutting out seawater might hurt the lagoon's fish and plant life. It is a case of saving a beautiful and special city while not harming the environment. Somehow, a balance between the two sides has to be worked out.

Boats carry people and goods.

Getting Around in Venice

Because cars aren't allowed in the city, there are only two ways of getting around. One is by walking. About 400 bridges cross the canals. The other popular form of transportation is by boat. Motor-powered water buses transport large numbers of people on the canals that run through Venice. Barges carry products to markets. Barges also carry garbage. Ambulance workers and police have their own boats.

Notes

Ancient Egypt

Zahi Hawass, right, discovered the mummy of a well-known governor. It was inside this limestone coffin.

PHOTOS: ZAHI HAWASS, COURTESY ABRAMS, PUBLISHER OF "VALLEY OF THE GOLDEN MUMMIES"

A F R I C A

Mediterranean Sea
PYRAMIDS OF GIZA Cairo
El Bawiti
Bahariya Oasis
Nile Red Sea
E G Y P T

How Mummies Were Made

The ancient Egyptians believed in life after death. But they also believed that a person couldn't live forever unless the dead body stayed in good condition. So Egyptians tried to preserve the bodies of the dead. These preserved bodies are called **mummies**. By studying mummies (and written records), today's scientists have learned how they were made.

In the Body

To make a mummy, priests first opened up the dead body. Then they removed most of its organs. Organs were dried and placed in special jars.

Next, the inside of the body was washed. It was also packed with linen or sawdust and sewn up. Then the body was covered in a powder called **natron**. It took 40 days for this salt-like substance to dry

out the body. Finally, the body was wrapped in linen bandages and put in a coffin.

Burying Mummies

A few mummies were placed in pyramids. But most were buried in special tombs. The ancient Egyptians knew what they were doing. Many of the discovered mummies have been in good condition.

This tomb held 42 mummies. Most were on shelves.

Meet a Mummy Expert

Zahi Hawass is an expert on mummies. He has spent much of his career exploring the mummy-filled tombs of the Bahariya Oasis in Egypt.

Curse of the Mummy?

When Hawass entered one of the tombs, a terrible smell was coming from a mysterious yellow powder on the floor. Just beyond the powder was the long-lost tomb of a well-known governor. He had ruled 25,000 years ago.

Scientists had searched 33 years for this tomb. Had some ancient Egyptian put the powder nearby to scare people away?

The governor's mummy was one of hundreds found at the oasis. Hawass believes there could be thousands more. Scientists hope to learn more about life in ancient Egypt by studying the mummies. What other secrets of Egyptian life do the mummies hold? Hawass and other researchers plan to spend many more years finding out.

Notes

THE NATION

Battling Over Alaska's Oil

Will oil rigs dot the landscape of a peaceful wildlife region?

By Terry McCarthy

Gwinch'in kids play outside in Arctic Village on the edge of the refuge.

Drilling is already allowed in Alaska's Prudhoe Bay. It gives 20 percent of U.S. oil. But many scientists say drilling can harm the environment.

Evon Peter stands on a hill and looks over an area of Alaska's snowy wilderness. Peter belongs to the Gwinch'in (Gway-chin) tribe. His tribe lives on the southern edge of the Arctic National Wildlife Refuge (ANWR).

Peter has a story for each part of the landscape. Many of his stories are about caribou, the wild reindeer his people depend on for food. "When I stand here, I feel I am free," he says.

Big changes may soon be coming to this quiet place, however. President George W. Bush, oil-industry leaders, and others want to drill for oil in the ANWR. They say drilling for oil there will help cut fuel prices. Drilling will also reduce America's need to buy oil from other nations. Alaska Senator Frank Murkowski has asked the Senate to pass a law that would allow the drilling.

Animal Worries

The ANWR was set aside for protection in 1960. Wildlife experts fear that drilling there could disturb polar bears and grizzlies. But their biggest worry is the caribou. More than 130,000 caribou travel each spring into a part called Area 1002 (see map).

The Gwinch'in people are against drilling. But many other Alaskans favor it. They say money from the sale of oil will improve their lives. Other critics say there might not even be much oil under the ANWR.

Few of the people who will make the decision to drill have ever seen the ANWR. Murkowski plans to take Senators there. Once they see this beautiful place, what will they decide to do?

Experts say drilling could hurt the polar bears that live in the refuge.

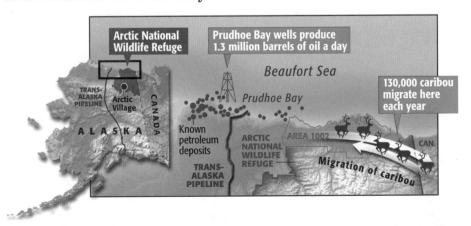

Arctic National Wildlife Refuge

Prudhoe Bay wells produce 1.3 million barrels of oil a day

Beaufort Sea

130,000 caribou migrate here each year

TRANS-ALASKA PIPELINE

Arctic Village

CANADA

Prudhoe Bay

Known petroleum deposits

ALASKA

ARCTIC NATIONAL WILDLIFE REFUGE

AREA 1002

CAN.

TRANS-ALASKA PIPELINE

Migration of caribou

Notes

NATIVE AMERICANS TODAY

Proud To Be Mohawk

These students speak only Mohawk in school.

About one in five Native Americans in the U.S. lives on reservations. Hundreds of years ago, Native Americans lost much of their land to European settlers and the government. In the 1800s, the government created reservations as places for Native Americans to live.

Losing the Ways of the Past

Native Americans who live on reservations aren't cut off from American life. Indians there speak English, watch TV, and share the same culture most other Americans do. This worries some Native Americans. They fear their languages and traditions will be lost. At first glance, their fears seem to have come true at the Freedom School in Rooseveltown, New York. Native American kids start their day the same way most students do—chatting about video games or movies. But when classes begin, their day takes on a different sound.

The children are learning Kanien'kehá:ka (Gah-nyah-gay-HA-gah). It is the language of their Native American ancestors, the Mohawk Indians. Most students are glad they are learning the langauge. They believe it helps them understand their Mohawk heritage better.

A School of Their Own

The Freedom School is on the U.S. side of the St. Regis reservation, which also has land in Canada. Parents started the Freedom School for preschoolers through eighth-graders in 1979. They wanted their children to learn the Mohawk language. Like many American Indian languages, Mohawk was disappearing.

A third-grader builds a paper model of a Mohawk longhouse. A longhouse was home to Mohawk people.

Students at the school also study Mohawk traditions. They sing old Mohawk songs and learn dances. They use native names. They are taught to be proud of who they are.

Native American Fact Sheet
- There are more than 2 million Native Americans in the U.S.
- California, Oklahoma, and Arizona have the most Native Americans.
- Nearly 1 out of every 100 people in the U.S. is a Native American.
- Native Americans belong to about 561 tribes.
- The biggest tribe is the Cherokee tribe of Oklahoma. It has a population of more than 300,000.

Mohawk Talk
The Mohawk and English languages have two big differences. The Mohawk language has fewer words than English. Also, certain letters in Mohawk are pronounced differently from English. For example, "wh" sounds like "f," "tsi" sounds like "j," and "r" sounds like "l." Here are a few words to get you started speaking Mohawk:
- hello: she:kon (*say-go*)
- bye: o:nem (*oh-nah*)
- mom: ista (*ee-stah*)
- dad: rakeni (*la*-gph-nee)
- friend: o:ri (*oh*-lee)

Notes

Energy:
Renewable and Nonrenewable Sources

Solar Panels

Without it, that flower outside your window wouldn't bloom. You wouldn't be able to travel to school. Buildings would be too hot or too cold. What is this force that helps all living things survive and perform daily activities? Energy.

What Is Energy?

Energy is the ability to do work and produce power. Energy helps run factories and provides heat and light in homes and schools. It also powers transportation (cars, trains, airplanes). The sources of this energy are fossil fuels, nuclear power, wind power, hydroelectric power (water), solar power (sun), geothermal energy (heat from within the Earth), and biomass (plants and grasses).

The Burning Problem

Power plants, industries, buildings, and motor vehicles burn mostly fossil fuels. These include coal, oil and gas. Fossil fuels are nonrenewable. That means supplies of them are limited and cannot be replaced.

Nuclear energy is another source of fuel. But producing nuclear energy creates dangerous radioactive wastes.

A Bright Future

Because we need energy to survive, it's important we use it responsibly. Renewable energy comes from such sources as sunlight, water, wind, geothermal energy and biomass. These forms of energy won't run out. They usually cause less pollution than nonrenewable energy. But no matter what source of energy you use, you can save energy by changing wasteful habits.

Wind Turbines

Saving Private Energy

One way to save resources is to make sure your home doesn't waste energy. If any of these energy-saving tips apply to your house, share them with your family.

- Having an attic without insulation lets lots of heat escape. An attic's insulation should be at least 12 inches thick.
- A furnace heats a house by burning gas or oil. But a furnace will use too much fuel if its filter is dirty. That's why the filter should be changed four or more times a year.
- The lights in some areas of a house, such as the kitchen, are turned on a lot. Replace one-quarter of the light bulbs in these areas with fluorescent bulbs. It will reduce energy used for lighting by 50 percent or more.
- A refrigerator uses a great deal of electricity. Be certain the door of the refrigerator closes tightly. Otherwise cold will escape. When that happens, the refrigerator uses even more electricity.
- The thermostat automatically sets the temperature in a house. To save energy in winter, set the thermostat at 70 degrees or lower. In summer, it should be set at 78 degrees or higher.

Notes

57

Barbara Jordan

Barbara Jordan was a pioneer in politics. She was an African American who fought for the underdog—because she, too, was an underdog for much of her life.

Barbara Jordan was born in Texas in 1936. Her family didn't have much money. But that didn't stop Jordan from doing well at school. She wanted to go to college at the University of Texas. But in those days most schools in the U.S., especially in the South, were segregated—they wouldn't allow blacks to attend classes with whites. For that reason, Jordan went to college at Texas Southern University. There, she learned to be a great speaker and debater.

After college, Jordan went on to become a lawyer. In 1961, she decided to run for the Texas State Senate. She won the election, becoming the first black woman to serve as a Texas State Senator. She quickly became a powerhouse at her job. But she wanted to do even more. So she ran for a bigger office—U.S. Congress.

Jordan Goes to Washington

In 1973, Jordan became the first black woman from the South to serve in the U.S. House of Representatives.

There Jordan became an important voice not only for African Americans, but for poor people of all races. She helped pass a law that helped injured workers. She was important in passing laws that let Mexican Americans and other minorities vote.

She's Number One!

As her fame grew, Jordan was called on for another first. She gave the keynote (main) speech at the Democratic National Convention in New York City. She was the first African-American woman to deliver this kind of speech. By then, Jordan was very popular. She was chosen in a poll as the number one woman people wanted to see as president. After 1979, Barbara decided

not to run for office. Instead, she taught at the University of Texas.

Over the years, Jordan fought for causes she believed in. One cause was showing that disabled people could perform well. By that time, Jordan herself was in a wheelchair. She had a disease that made it difficult for her to walk. In 1994, she was awarded the Medal of Freedom for all her work. This medal is the highest honor the country can give a citizen.

Jordan said, "What the people want is simple. They want an America as good as its promise." Jordan worked her whole life toward that goal. She died in 1996, and remains an inspiration to all Americans.